Contents

What Was
the Harlem
Renaissance?

by Sherri L. Smith

illustrated by Tim Foley

Penguin Workshop

To the artists working for a better world—
past, present, and future—SLS

For Keenan and Lydia—TF

PENGUIN WORKSHOP
An imprint of Penguin Random House LLC, New York

First published in the United States of America by Penguin Workshop,
an imprint of Penguin Random House LLC, New York, 2021

Visit us online at penguinrandomhouse.com.

Library of Congress Control Number: 2021020890

Printed in the United States of America

ISBN 9780593225905 (paperback)   10 9 8 7 6 5 4 3 2 1 WOR
ISBN 9780593225912 (library binding)   10 9 8 7 6 5 4 3 2 1 WOR

What Was the Harlem Renaissance?

It was summertime in Toluca, Mexico, in 1920. An American teenager named Langston Hughes and his father were leading two horses across the lonesome countryside. Langston's father was an engineer. He wanted his son to become one, too. Engineers made good money.

Langston had seen what it was like to be both rich and poor. He had lived with his mother's family in the midwestern United States and on his father's ranch in Mexico. His father had money. His mother did not. Black people

were segregated from white people in the United States. (*Segregated* means kept separate.) African Americans did not have the same opportunities as white Americans. That was one reason Langston's father lived in Mexico. He thought

Langston would have a better life as an engineer outside the United States. But Langston had other ideas.

Langston loved to write. He desperately wanted to go to New York City's uptown neighborhood

of Harlem. The bustling African American community was like a city within a city. Black writers and artists were beginning to make a name for themselves there. Langston would later say, "I dreamt about Harlem."

In June 1921, the *Crisis* magazine published Langston's first poem. It was called "The Negro Speaks of Rivers." (*Negro* is an outdated term for people of Black African descent.) The poem was about the journey of Black people from Africa to the American South.

"Did they pay you anything?" he remembered his father asking. No, Langston admitted. But it was a start. Not long after, his father agreed to pay for college in New York. Langston was headed to Harlem! He was only nineteen years old. Soon he would become one of the best-known poets of the Harlem Renaissance.

The Harlem Renaissance was a tremendous wave of creativity in the Black community of New York City. It took place during the 1920s and 1930s. African American culture had long been looked down on in the United States. Now new Black music, poetry, novels, dance, and art challenged those old views.

The Italian Renaissance

The word *renaissance* is French for "rebirth." It means an age of growth in arts and sciences. The original Renaissance began in fourteenth-century Florence, Italy, when new ideas in science and art spread across Europe. There was a renewed interest in the great works of ancient Greek and Roman thinkers. This knowledge had been lost to Western Europe for many hundreds of years. Some of the most famous names of the Italian Renaissance are Leonardo da Vinci, Michelangelo, and Galileo.

Black artists began to take inspiration from their African roots and everyday lives. They wanted to express themselves not just as Americans but as

African Americans. And it all began in Harlem, what Langston Hughes called "the greatest Negro city in the world."

CHAPTER 1
Welcome to Harlem!

Harlem of the 1920s was home to a swiftly growing African American community on the 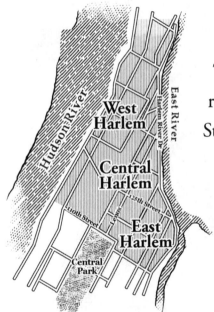 island of Manhattan in New York City. This "city within a city" reached from 110th Street all the way up to 144th Street between Lenox Avenue on the east and Seventh Avenue on the west. Famous nightclubs like the Cotton Club and the Savoy Ballroom studded Lenox Avenue like neon jewels. They attracted wealthy customers and celebrities. Secret nightclubs called speakeasies served the Black working class on 133rd Street. On Seventh Avenue,

The Savoy Ballroom

Smalls' Paradise offered "A Red Hot Show in a Cool Place" to racially mixed crowds. Smalls' was a favorite hangout of the Harlem Renaissance set and featured dancing waiters!

Harlem wasn't just about nightlife. The 135th Street branch of the New York Public Library and the Harlem branch of the YMCA held many cultural events.

135th Street branch of the New York Public Library

Prohibition (1919–1933)

In 1919, an *amendment*—a change—to the Constitution made it illegal to sell or make any kind of alcohol for drinking. That marked the beginning of Prohibition, which went into effect the next year. (*Prohibition* means forbidding something.) But many people found ways around this law. Bars called speakeasies opened, which served liquor. These bars were kept a secret. A password was needed to enter. In some speakeasies, customers were entertained by jazz bands. Prohibition ended on December 5, 1933, but people continued to listen to the upbeat, swinging music heard in those bars.

The famous Apollo Theater on 125th Street near the local shopping district opened its doors to Black audiences in 1934. It draws African American performers from around the country to this day.

Harlem was a thriving neighborhood with

Black doctors, lawyers, and even police officers. Wealthy areas like Strivers' Row and Sugar Hill boasted stately stone townhouses and elegant apartment buildings. The sense of possibility in Harlem drew newcomers by the thousands. But it had not always been that way.

Houses in Sugar Hill

In the 1800s, Harlem had been a fashionable white neighborhood. By the end of the century, a large number of Jewish immigrants had moved in. The famous magician Harry Houdini bought a home there in 1904.

Harry Houdini

That same year, an enterprising African American man named Philip A. Payton Jr. began buying property in Harlem. "My first opportunity came as a result of a dispute between two white landlords in West 134th Street," Payton recalled. "To 'get even' one of them turned his house over to me to fill with colored tenants," he said. (*Colored* is an outdated word for people with brown skin.)

Philip Payton

Payton was a smart businessman. He soon opened the Afro-American Realty Company to sell houses and rent apartments to Black people in Harlem. At the time, that was about four thousand people. By 1930, Harlem stretched north to 155th Street and south to 114th Street, and 165,000 Black people called it home!

CHAPTER 2
Changing Times

Why did the Harlem Renaissance take place in the 1920s and '30s? The previous decade was a time of great change in America. Millions of African Americans from the South began moving North where they hoped to find a better life.

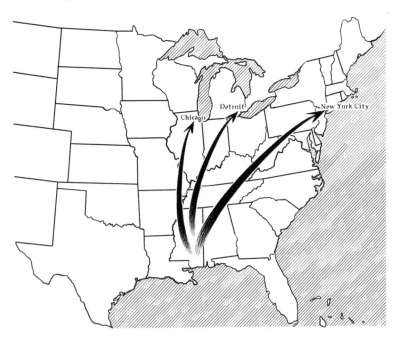

In the South, Black people had been forced to live under conditions that made it nearly impossible for them to get a good education or job, or to feel safe. So they left for cities such as New York and settled in certain neighborhoods, such as Harlem. These neighborhoods became thriving African American communities where Black culture flourished.

Then came World War I and with it, even more change. In 1917, the United States entered the war in Europe. In the United States, some white Americans didn't think Black people were as brave or intelligent as white people. Many Black men thought fighting in the war was a chance to show that those ideas were wrong! They hoped that by serving in Europe with honor they would be rewarded with equal treatment back home. None fought more nobly than the men of the 369th Regiment.

The Great Migration

Although slavery ended in the United States in 1865, many African Americans continued to be mistreated because of the color of their skin. Southern states created laws, known as Jim Crow laws, that made sure Black people couldn't vote and were segregated from white people. African Americans couldn't eat in the same restaurants, stay in the same hotels, or even drink from the same

water fountains. These same laws failed to protect the lives of Black people. Many innocent African Americans were murdered, or lynched, by white mobs. Their killers were allowed to go free.

From 1915 to 1970, around six million Black people left the South to find a better life. This is known as the Great Migration. (*Migration* means to move from one place to another.) Many African Americans settled in big cities like New York, Chicago, Philadelphia, and Detroit.

Soldiers from the 369th Regiment

The 369th served in France, fighting against the Germans. Of all the American regiments its size, the 369th spent the most time on the battlefield. And they suffered the most losses.

World War I

In 1914, an Austrian archduke and his wife were shot and killed. Their murders ignited World War I with the Central Powers (Germany, Austria-Hungary, Turkey, and Bulgaria) fighting against the Allies (France, Great Britain, Italy, Russia,

Austrian archduke Franz Ferdinand and his wife

Romania, Japan, and, eventually, the United States).

The United States entered the conflict in 1917 after German submarines began sinking American ships. Ultimately, over two million American troops were sent to France to turn back the German invasion. Among them were the Harlem Hellfighters. The war ended late in 1918 with an Allied victory.

The 369th fought so fiercely that the Germans reportedly called them "hellfighters." Both the United States and France awarded the "Harlem Hellfighters" medals for their brave service.

Croix de Guerre medal

African American soldiers were treated with respect in France. They were not turned away from restaurants and hotels the way they would have been in the States.

A few months after the war was won, 2,900 Harlem Hellfighters marched up Fifth Avenue in New York City. The front page of the *New York Times* newspaper declared, "Fifth Av. Cheers Negro Veterans." Photographs show the soldiers in their domed helmets, rifles at their sides.

It was an impressive display of African American pride. The Hellfighters were celebrating a double victory—one over the Germans, and one over racism at home. Or so they thought.

The Germans had indeed been defeated. But racism in the United States had not. Many white Americans viewed these heroic Black soldiers as a threat. In 1919, in cities across the country, white people attacked African Americans in violent race riots known as "Red Summer."

Claude McKay

The attacks inspired poet Claude McKay's poem "If We Must Die." It urged Black people to fight back with dignity. McKay later became a famous poet of the Harlem Renaissance.

Sadly, the riots continued. By the end of the year, hundreds of African Americans lay dead and thousands more were houseless. It was clear America was at a terrible crossroads. The old stereotypes of Jim Crow and the false belief in white superiority had to be erased.

Could art be the answer?

CHAPTER 3
On with the Show!

By 1920, Harlem had become a destination for upwardly mobile Black people. It was seen as a place where great things could happen. This hopeful energy was what attracted Langston Hughes to Harlem. That, and a musical called *Shuffle Along*.

The show opened on May 23, 1921, at the 63rd Street Music

Hall on Broadway. (Broadway is the name of the theater district in New York City.) James Hubert "Eubie" Blake and Noble Sissle teamed up to

Eubie Blake

Noble Sissle

create the show. Sissle had been a Harlem Hellfighter. Blake had worked with ragtime musician James Europe. Blake and Sissle believed the best way to appeal to a wider audience—both Black and white theatergoers—was with a musical comedy. *Shuffle Along* would prove them right!

Shuffle Along told the story of two dishonest grocery store owners who run for mayor in a fictional town only to be defeated by an honest man. Blake composed the music. Sissle wrote the lyrics, the words to songs. While it might seem outdated today, the show was groundbreaking for its time. It featured an all-Black cast, toe-tapping music, singing, dancing, laughs, and a realistic love story. Up until this point, all African American onstage romances had been played for humor.

Florence Mills

The star was a famous singer. Florence Mills had a unique voice, "full of bubbling, bell-like, bird-like tones." One of the show's songs, "I'm Just Wild About Harry," was a massive hit and years later became President Harry Truman's campaign theme. (And he won!)

The hit show ran for more than five hundred performances—a record for a show written, produced, performed, and directed entirely by African Americans. *Shuffle Along*'s popularity sparked new interest in African American culture. Over the next three years, nine other Black musicals were created for Broadway. It also helped desegregate Broadway audiences. Black theatergoers could sit in seats near the stage that had been for "whites only."

Langston Hughes was a broke college student. He didn't mind sitting in the cheap seats night after night to hear Mills sing. To him *Shuffle Along* "gave just the proper push . . . to that Negro vogue of the 20's, that spread to books, African sculpture, music, and dancing." (*Vogue* means fashion.)

The Cotton Club

White people began flooding north to Harlem for Black entertainment. Unfortunately, even in Harlem, some famous nightclubs had "whites only" policies. The Cotton Club was even designed to look like an old southern plantation. Great African American musicians and singers performed there. But Black customers were only allowed inside if they were famous. And even then, they had to sit to the side.

African Americans were not welcome in most restaurants or nightclubs in white neighborhoods. One exception was the Civic Club of New York in lower Manhattan. It would host one of the most important events in the Harlem Renaissance.

CHAPTER 4
A Night to Remember

March 21, 1924, was a windy Friday in New York City. The forecast was for snow. But the atmosphere at 14 West Twelfth Street was warm and lively. The building was the home of the Civic Club. The Club had been founded in 1917 with the goal of improving society. It was unusual for its day in that it welcomed both Black and white members. That evening, guests of both races stepped through the doorway and into history. Their host was Charles S. Johnson.

Johnson was the editor of a Black magazine called *Opportunity*. The night's event was to celebrate the release of Jessie Redmon

Jessie Redmon Fauset

Fauset's first novel, *There Is Confusion*. It was about

three childhood friends dealing with adulthood. Unlike other books of the time, these Black characters were not poor or working-class. They were middle-class, like Fauset herself.

But what had been intended as a small gathering at the Civic Club that night bloomed into a crowd of over one hundred.

The master of ceremonies was Alain Locke. Locke was a respected writer and educator. Born in Philadelphia, he earned two degrees at Harvard University. The events of the evening would help shape his ideas about what he called "the New Negro."

Alain Locke

According to Locke, America had treated "the Old Negro" as a problem to be "kept down" and put "in his place." But the New Negro took pride in being Black and was a vibrant participant in society. Part of that participation was in the creative arts.

Many historians today consider the Civic Club event the official birthday party for the Harlem Renaissance. Guests gave speeches about the need for writers who could show the richness of African American life.

A. Philip Randolph (left) and W.E.B. Du Bois (right)

The editors of important Black-run magazines were also present. Civil rights activist W.E.B. Du Bois had started the *Crisis*. Another activist, A. Philip Randolph, cofounded the *Messenger*.

These magazines helped build the careers of young Black writers and artists. They often held contests with prize money to help struggling authors earn a living.

Through newspapers and magazines, new voices in Harlem could reach more readers. Langston Hughes attempted to start his own

magazine in 1926 with writer Zora Neale Hurston and others. It was called *Fire!!* Unfortunately, they could only afford to print the first issue. And most of those burned up in an actual house fire!

Wealthy white patrons of the arts, book publishers, and editors were invited to the Civic Club party in the hope that they would help the new writers. At the end of the night, the white editor of a magazine called *Survey Graphic* invited Locke to create an entire issue about the New Negro. The Harlem Renaissance had begun!

CHAPTER 5
New Voices

In March 1925, *Survey Graphic* magazine published a special issue, "Harlem: Mecca of the New Negro." (A *mecca* means an important gathering place.) Alain Locke later expanded the issue into a book called *The New Negro: Voices of the Harlem Renaissance*. Both the book and the magazine issue featured writers and artists who would go on to have long, well-regarded careers.

Jessie Redmon Fauset, the guest of honor at the Civic Club party, contributed an essay on Black comedies to Locke's book. Fauset left her job as a teacher in Washington, DC. She moved to Harlem to become the literary editor of the *Crisis*. There she helped discover many writers

of the period. She was the editor who published Langston Hughes's first poem! Fauset also went on to write three more novels as well as poetry, short stories, and essays.

Fauset also hosted literary salons, or parties where artists gathered.

After Fauset left the *Crisis*, she was unable to find work in publishing. She married and returned to teaching. Fauset was living in Philadelphia when she died in 1961.

Several of Langston Hughes's poems appeared in *The New Negro*. But it was his poem "The Weary Blues" that made a real splash in 1925. It's about an old musician playing the blues on Lenox Avenue in Harlem. Its sorrowful tone captures both the feel of the music and of the way people in Harlem spoke. The poem won first prize at an Opportunity Awards dinner. Still, the honor was not enough to live on. For that, Hughes would need to make an even bigger splash.

Langston Hughes receiving an *Opportunity* magazine poetry prize

Hughes moved to Washington, DC, in 1924 to live with his mother. He had left college and was working as a busboy, clearing tables in a hotel restaurant. One day he spotted a famous white poet named Vachel Lindsay dining there and took a chance.

Rent Parties

During the Great Migration, Black people left behind lives as poor farmers, hoping to find better jobs in big neighborhoods like Harlem. Apartment buildings soon became overcrowded. Landlords responded by dividing rooms into smaller spaces and raising the rent. In order to make ends meet, people in Harlem often threw rent parties.

Hosts would place cards advertising the event in the elevators of their buildings. The cards often began with a rhyme like, "Some wear pajamas,

An invitation card for a rent party

some wear pants, what does it matter just so you can dance." Guests would pay a small fee to join in the fun. Cheap drinks, food, and live music were the attraction. If the party was big enough, the host would earn enough money to pay their rent for the month.

As Harlem nightspots became more popular with white visitors, the rent party became a "place to have a drink that the tourist hadn't yet discovered," Langston Hughes recalled. He kept the invitation cards because he was "intrigued by the little rhymes at the top." Later he said of the parties, "I can still hear their laughter in my ears, hear the soft slow music, and feel the floor shaking as the dancers danced."

Hughes boldly slipped three of his poems onto Lindsay's table. The poet was so impressed by the poetry that he told the newspapers about it! Soon Hughes's photo appeared in papers around the country. It was great publicity!

One of Hughes's best-known poems is called "Harlem." It is about what happens to frustrated hopes. It begins with the line, "What happens to a dream deferred?" (*Deferred* means delayed.) Although he's most famous for his poetry, Hughes also wrote novels, short stories, essays, and plays.

Zora Neale Hurston was a friend of Langston Hughes who knew how to chase dreams! One of her short stories was featured in *The New Negro*. Hurston was born in Alabama and grew up in Florida. Her mother died when Hurston was only thirteen. Life was hard but her mother had told her to jump at the sun. "We might not land on the sun," Hurston said, "but at least we

Zora Neale Hurston

would get off the ground." Hurston jumped high. She ended up studying at Howard University, a historically Black school in Washington, DC. The school's literary magazine published her first story. She also joined a literary club started by two professors. One of them was Alain Locke.

In 1925, Hurston moved to New York and became part of the Harlem literary set. But what Hurston really wanted was to be an anthropologist. (Anthropologists study human behavior as well as societies both past and present.) This interest was reflected in Hurston's work. She had a good ear for language. She wrote the way everyday Black people spoke. In 1927, Hurston began collecting Black folktales in Florida that would later become a book called *Mules and Men*. In 1936, she was awarded money to study folklore in Jamaica and Haiti. During this time, she wrote her best-known novel,

Their Eyes Were Watching God. It tells the story of a hopeful young Black woman from Florida. Some consider it one of the most important novels of the twentieth century.

Several poems and an essay on music written by Claude McKay were published in *The New Negro.* Jamaican-born McKay had lived in the American South. It was there that he first experienced "intensely bitter" racism, he later

wrote. In 1914, he moved north to New York. He said Harlem was "like entering a paradise of my own people."

Langston Hughes wrote in a loose style sometimes called "jazz poetry." McKay, however, used traditional forms of poetry like the sonnet to write about inequality. McKay traveled the world speaking out against American racism. He wrote several novels, essays, and articles on Black life in America. He died in Chicago in 1948.

Each of these writers were just part of the voice of the New Negro. Although their styles of writing were different, they spoke with a new pride in being themselves. Black, educated, well traveled, and outspoken, the New Negro had arrived. And not just through the written word.

Arthur Schomburg (1874–1938)

Arthur Schomburg wasn't a writer or an artist. However, he played an important part in the Harlem Renaissance. He was born Arturo Alfonso Schomburg in Puerto Rico to parents of African and German descent. When Schomburg was a child, a teacher told him Black people had no history. Schomburg set out to prove his teacher wrong. He became a historian! The essay he contributed to *The New Negro* was about understanding the past.

Schomburg moved to New York in 1891 when he was seventeen. In the 1920s, he began collecting works by African Americans. By 1926, he had over five thousand books, three thousand documents, and two thousand pieces of art created by Black people! Schomburg's collection became the basis of the Schomburg Center for Research in Black Culture that remains in Harlem to this day.

CHAPTER 6
All That Jazz

Thanks to the Harlem Renaissance, jazz was sweeping the nation in the 1920s. The decade became known as the Jazz Age. Jazz is a uniquely African American music born from Black folk music and another style, called ragtime.

Ragtime was created by Black musicians in the late 1800s. It is usually played on the piano and features a *syncopated* rhythm. (*Syncopated* means that it does not follow an expected beat.) The left hand plays a steady rhythm like European classical music. The right hand plays a "ragged" rhythm. The result is lively, swinging music with bounce. Two famous ragtime pieces are "Maple Leaf Rag" and "The Entertainer."

Scott Joplin, who wrote "The Entertainer" and "Maple Leaf Rag"

Jazz inherited ragtime's syncopated rhythm. But it has a looser feel. Jazz musicians often follow their own mood or imagination. As a result, jazz is never played the same way twice. Jazz music appeared in places like New Orleans, Chicago, and New York City. It set toes tapping around the world!

One of the fathers of ragtime and jazz was WWI Harlem Hellfighter James Reese Europe. Originally from Alabama, he became a popular bandleader and composer in New York City. Europe's orchestra bridged the gap between ragtime and jazz. During World War I, his music started a jazz craze in France.

James Reese Europe and his band

Europe also broke down barriers preventing Black musicians from playing in whites-only clubs. He did this by teaming up his band with a famous white dance act—Vernon and Irene Castle. The Castles' popularity meant Europe's band appeared before many white audiences.

Between dance numbers, the band often played a song called "The Memphis Blues." It was written by a musician named W.C. Handy, who was also from Alabama. Handy and Europe were two of the best-known Black musicians of the day.

Handy's nickname was "Father of the Blues."

The blues is another popular type of Black music with roots in African American spirituals (religious songs). The blues often tells stories of heartache and lost love. The Castles liked "Memphis Blues" so much that they created a new dance for it called the foxtrot that's still popular in ballroom dancing today.

Noble Sissle (of *Shuffle Along* fame) had been part of Europe's Harlem Hellfighters band. Sissle once told Handy about being sent to play for wounded soldiers during the war. Reportedly, "when the band struck up the blues the American doughboys tossed away their crutches, danced and hobbled, yelling, 'They're from home! They're from home!'"

Europe's band was one of the first Black groups to record their music. Records had a huge impact in introducing Black musicians to white people. In 1920, a woman named Mamie Smith recorded a song called "Crazy Blues." Previously, Black musicians were only recorded

if their music appealed to white listeners. "Crazy Blues" was the first record by a Black singer that was made for Black audiences. And it was a hit!

By 1923, Black jazz records were among the most popular in the country. New names like

Mamie Smith performing

Duke Ellington and Cab Calloway appeared on the scene. Edward "Duke" Ellington earned his nickname for his gentlemanly manners. Born in Washington, DC, in 1899, he started playing piano when he was seven. As a teenager, he composed his first song, "Soda Fountain Rag." Ellington moved to Harlem in 1923. By 1927, he was leading his own orchestra at the Cotton Club. One of his most popular jazz pieces is "Take the 'A' Train," written by Billy Strayhorn. The title refers to the subway line in New York City that runs through Harlem.

Duke Ellington

Cabell "Cab" Calloway III was born in Rochester, New York, in 1907. Calloway started law school in Chicago, but left to become a singer. In 1929, he moved to Harlem. Two years later, his orchestra was also playing at the Cotton Club. Calloway was known for his white tuxedos, floppy hair, big singing voice, and noodle-limbed dancing. His best-known song is "Minnie the Moocher."

Cab Calloway

Because the Cotton Club was segregated, most African Americans rarely got to see some of the greatest Black musicians perform. Records and the radio helped fill in this gap.

And so did national tours. The popularity of the music meant Black orchestras were booked to play for white audiences. Even so, on the road the musicians were often barred from hotels and restaurants because of their skin color. And once white bands began to copy Black music, they were often hired instead of African American bands.

Another big name in jazz was Fletcher Henderson. Henderson's band was extremely popular, especially after a new trumpet player joined in 1924. His name was Louis Armstrong. Armstrong had grown up a poor kid in New Orleans. His puff-cheeked trumpet playing earned him the nickname "Satchmo" for "Satchel Mouth." Armstrong liked to improvise. He became known for his "fluid technique and dazzling high notes," according to one scholar. He also sang with a distinctive warm and gravelly voice that made scat singing popular.

Scat is a style of singing nonsense syllables that express feeling through sound rather than words. Armstrong went on to become one of the most important jazz musicians in the world. His song "What a Wonderful World" is still popular today.

Two other famous singers of the Harlem Renaissance were Bessie Smith and Ethel Waters. Smith was known as "Empress of the Blues." She was one of the highest paid singers of her time. Ethel Waters was known for her warm, emotional voice. She started singing in church choirs in Philadelphia when she was only five years old. As a teenager, she performed under the name "Sweet Mama Stringbean." Waters became a sensation after singing W.C. Handy's "St. Louis Blues." Once she moved to Harlem in 1919, she gained even greater fame as an actress. But it was music that had put her in the spotlight.

Ethel Waters

From ragtime to the blues and jazz, African American music holds a place of special cultural importance. To this day, jazz is considered to be a uniquely American art form.

CHAPTER 7
Artists of the Renaissance

Music and writing traveled more easily than heavy sculptures and paintings. Perhaps that is why the fine art made during the Harlem Renaissance took longer to reach the general public. Black magazines helped change that by showcasing the work of new artists. Much of the art in the "Harlem" issue of *Survey Graphic* was by a white  German illustrator named Fritz Winold Reiss. But when Locke created *The New Negro* book later that year, Reiss suggested the "pictures should be done by a Negro." Enter Aaron Douglas.

Aaron Douglas

Douglas had been working as a high school art teacher in Kansas. It was that "spectacular issue of *Survey Graphic*" that made him decide to come to New York. Once there, he studied with Reiss. Douglas went on to become one of the best-known Black artists of his day.

Douglas's drawings were influenced by African art. He contrasted sharp black figures against white backgrounds inspired by African tribal imagery. Douglas went on to illustrate Black magazines like *Opportunity* as well as the white-owned *Vanity Fair*. He is perhaps best known for four large murals called *Aspects of Negro Life*, still on display at the public library in Harlem now known as the Schomburg Center.

Aaron Douglas's *Aspects of Negro Life: The Negro in an African Setting*

The wall-size paintings were created in 1934 as part of a government project to support the arts. They show the journey of African Americans from Africa, through slavery in America, and ultimately to freedom.

Augusta Savage was a sculptor who had to fight to make art. As a child in Florida, she made ducks and chickens out of clay. But her father disapproved. He "almost whipped all the art out of me," she recalled. But that did not stop her. Winning a prize at a county fair gave her the courage to keep sculpting and, eventually, to move to Harlem.

Savage began to sculpt busts of famous Black people, including W.E.B. Du Bois and political activist Marcus Garvey. (A *bust* is a likeness of a person's head and chest.) She sculpted African Americans with warmth and beauty. *Gamin* is based on her nephew. It was featured on the cover of *Opportunity* in 1929. The piece won a cash prize that helped her pay for a trip to Europe to study classical art. When she returned, she started an art school in Harlem. There, Savage offered free lessons and invited important people like Arthur Schomburg to serve as models for the students. She said, "If I can inspire one of these youngsters to develop the talent I know they possess, then my monument will be in their work."

The WPA

In 1929, the United States' economy collapsed.
The next ten years became known as the Great
Depression. Businesses failed and millions of

Franklin D. Roosevelt

people lost their jobs
and homes. In order to
help, President Franklin D.
Roosevelt started a group
of programs called the New
Deal. It included the Works
Progress Administration.
The WPA helped create jobs
for artists and writers.

Thanks to programs like the WPA, Aaron Douglas
created his famous set of murals. It enabled Zora
Neal Hurston to travel to Florida to collect African
American folktales. It also funded the Harlem
Community Art Center, which Augusta Savage ran.

In 1937, Savage was asked to create a piece for the 1939 New York World's Fair. *The Harp* was a sixteen-foot sculpture of African American singers shaped to look like the strings of the instrument. Unfortunately, the piece was made of plaster and destroyed after the fair ended. That same year, Savage opened the first art gallery in the United States started by a Black

Meta Vaux Warrick Fuller

woman showcasing Black artists. It featured another Black female sculptor, Meta Vaux Warrick Fuller.

Fuller was already an established artist by the 1920s. Like Savage, she had also studied in Europe. Fuller trained with the world-famous French sculptor Auguste Rodin. She created large statues in bronze, like Rodin's *The Thinker*. Fuller's own masterpiece was *Ethiopia*. It's a bronze of an Ethiopian woman wrapped toe to waist like a mummy. But her arms and head are free. Fuller said the piece represented the Black community, "who had once made history and now after a long sleep was awaking, gradually unwinding the bandage of its mummied past." For some, this single piece of art represents the Harlem Renaissance.

James Van Der Zee

Fuller worked in clay and plaster; James Van Der Zee worked with light. As a teenager, Van Der Zee won a camera in a contest in Massachusetts. He moved to Harlem in 1906. In 1916, he opened a photography studio with his wife. Over the next four decades, Van Der Zee created portraits of celebrities as well as scenes of everyday life in Harlem. But as personal cameras became more popular, people began taking their own family photos and Van Der Zee's portrait work was almost forgotten. Fortunately, he was rediscovered in the 1960s. In 1979, President Jimmy Carter honored Van Der Zee with the Library of Congress Living Legacy award.

By the mid-1930s, art was alive and thrumming across Harlem. In addition to Savage's school, students could take classes at the Harlem YMCA and the library. Charles Alston and Henry W. Bannarn started a studio in 1934 at 306 West 141st Street. Known as 306, the studio became "the main center in Harlem for creative Black people in all the arts." The energy of this period would carry into the next decade and beyond, inspiring a new generation of artists.

CHAPTER 8
Stars of Stage and Screen

Before television existed, Americans flocked to the theater and movies for entertainment. Even in the worst years of the Great Depression, people would spend what little money they had to see a movie. (Movies were also cheaper back them.) But it wasn't until the Harlem Renaissance that Black actors gained more attention.

In 1927, the singer Ethel Waters starred in a show on Broadway called *Africana*. Six years later, she became the first African American performer to receive equal billing with white actors, for the Broadway show *As Thousands Cheer*. Soon she was among the highest-paid actresses on Broadway! Later, she became the first African American to star in her own TV sitcom, *Beulah*, in 1950.

The role she played was a stereotype—a maid working for a white family. But Waters gave depth to the part. She eventually became the first Black person to be nominated for television's biggest award, an Emmy. She was also nominated for the biggest movie award, an Oscar.

Ethel Waters in *Beulah*

Florence Mills, the star of *Shuffle Along*, was a triple threat! (A *triple threat* is someone who can do three types of work very well. Mills could dance, act, and sing.) She was wildly popular. She performed in Europe and another show, *Blackbirds*, was created just for her. Mills chose to do all-Black shows to give work to more African American performers. Two *Shuffle Along* cast members benefited from this—Josephine Baker and Paul Robeson.

Josephine Baker was also a triple threat. She was only a teenager when she performed in *Shuffle Along*. She found even greater success in France performing her famous "Danse Sauvage," or savage dance, wearing a skirt of bananas! Baker went on to appear in movies, concerts, and dance performances in Europe and the United States. During World War II, she even worked as a spy helping the French! She risked her life gathering important information that helped free her adopted country from the Nazis.

Josephine Baker

Paul Robeson was the son of a well-to-do mother and a man who had escaped slavery. Robeson quit his job as a lawyer in New York City because of racism and became an actor. Robeson is famous for playing the lead in Shakespeare's *Othello*.

The famous role of a Black king was usually played by white men wearing dark makeup.

Paul Robeson as Othello

Robeson also starred in a movie called *The Emperor Jones*. But he is perhaps best known for singing "Ol' Man River" in *Show Boat* on Broadway and in the movie that followed.

Robeson's first movie role was thanks to a Black filmmaker named Oscar Micheaux. White producers in Hollywood usually only cast Black actors as servants or enslaved people. But Micheaux made movies by and about all kinds of Black people. Micheaux was a farmer when he wrote a novel called *The Homesteader*. Based on his life, it tells the story

Oscar Micheaux

of a Black farmer who falls in love with a white woman but cannot marry her because they are not of the same race. Micheaux sold the book door-to-door. An African American film company wanted to turn the story into a movie. Micheaux decided to do it himself! He ultimately made over forty films for Black audiences. In 1948, his final film, *The Betrayal*, became the first Black-made movie to play in white theaters.

Tap dancer Bill "Bojangles" Robinson was another triple threat, and another Harlem Hellfighter! He was the drum major who led James Europe's band up Fifth Avenue in 1919. Robinson started dancing when he was only five years old. He appeared on Broadway in *Blackbirds* in 1928. Robinson went on to make several movies, most famously with white child star Shirley Temple.

Unfortunately, roles for African Americans in Hollywood movies remained very limited. Especially in the South, white audiences were not

Bill Robinson tap-dancing

interested in seeing Black characters on screen unless they were servants. Hattie McDaniel won an Oscar for best supporting actress in 1940. She played an enslaved maid in the movie *Gone with the Wind*. It would be another twenty-four years before a second Black actor won—this time for best actor. In his acceptance speech, Sidney Poitier said, "It is a long journey to this moment." The journey for equal representation in the movies continues to this day.

Hattie McDaniel with her Oscar

CHAPTER 9
The End . . . and After

The Great Depression signaled the beginning of the end for the Harlem Renaissance. Langston Hughes said, "We were no longer in vogue, anyway, we Negroes. . . . Colored actors began to go hungry, publishers politely rejected new manuscripts, and patrons found other uses for their money." Magazines like the *Crisis* and *Opportunity* stopped giving out cash prizes to writers. The WPA provided work for some for a few years. But most Black writers and artists of the day lived hand-to-mouth.

As time passed, popular interest in Black culture began to fade. Struggling Americans were more concerned with money than with art. Hughes said, "The ordinary Negroes hadn't heard of the Negro Renaissance. And if they had, it hadn't raised their wages any." Even Alain Locke realized the New Negro movement "should have addressed itself more to the people themselves."

Black people kept arriving from the South looking for work. But jobs were scarce during the Great Depression. It was lack of work that struck the final blow to the Harlem Renaissance in March 1935, in the form of a riot.

Many Harlem businesses had remained white owned. They made their money from Black customers but refused to hire Black employees. The community had peacefully protested this unfair treatment. Tensions were still high when

a sixteen-year-old Black Puerto Rican boy was accused of stealing from a store. After his arrest, a false rumor spread that the boy had been killed.

That led to a riot. The poet Claude McKay later called it "the gesture of despair of a bewildered, baffled, and disillusioned people." By the time it was over, more than a hundred people were in jail, thirty went to the hospital, and three were dead.

The Harlem Renaissance was born from the hope that art could help gain equality for African Americans. The riot seemed to prove that its efforts had failed to change the lives of everyday people. The neighborhood fell on hard times that would last many years.

But all was not lost. After all, a renaissance is a rebirth.

The Harlem Renaissance gave birth to the New Negro. That spirit lived on in the works of future Black writers such as James Baldwin and Lorraine Hansberry, who in turn influence writers today.

James Baldwin

Lorraine Hansberry

And each new generation of writers has claimed a wider audience among Americans of all races.

Many in the Harlem Renaissance went on to join the civil rights movement of the 1950s and 1960s. Louis Armstrong donated money to the cause and spoke out against segregation in schools.

One of the organizers of the famous March on Washington, DC, in 1963 was the *Messenger* magazine editor A. Philip Randolph. Josephine Baker shared the stage with Martin Luther King that day. She spoke briefly, saying, "I have walked into the palaces of kings and queens and into the houses of presidents. . . . But I could not walk into a hotel in America and get a cup of coffee."

Toward the end of the march, Dr. King delivered his famous "I Have a Dream" speech. King was a fan of Langston Hughes's poetry. Some people believe his speech was inspired in part by Hughes's line, "What happens to a dream deferred?" In his speech, King talks about his dream for equality. He said that he was "personally the victim of deferred dreams." But he still believed his dream could come true.

Music also outlived the Harlem Renaissance. Jazz continues to influence modern music, including hip-hop. One musician said, "Hip-hop is like one of the children of jazz." Another musician called both types of music "a link to the reality of Black folks and Black youth in particular."

Hip-hop artist Kendrick Lamar

The art of the Harlem Renaissance also inspired new generations of African American visual artists. Augusta Savage's student Jacob Lawrence and 306 Group member Romare Bearden both went on to great fame as part of a second wave of Harlem artists. Their Renaissance origins are powerfully reflected in their work.

During the Harlem Renaissance, it was illegal

A painting by Jacob Lawrence from his series The Great Migration

for people who were attracted to people of their same sex to live openly in America. But this did not stop artists such as Langston Hughes, Alain Locke, and Countee Cullen from including those experiences in their work. They are now celebrated for presenting a little-seen part of Black life in America.

In the first quarter of the twenty-first century, Harlem itself began experiencing another rebirth. More people of all races have moved to the area. A vibrant new culture is bringing the famous neighborhood and its history back to life.

The Harlem Renaissance set out to celebrate African American culture. In that, it succeeded. Even so, African Americans and other people of color still struggle for equality in society and the creative arts. The movie industry has come under fire for its lack of diversity. The same is true in the visual arts and the book world. But efforts are being made to improve representation. And African Americans continue to make beautiful art despite the challenges they face. That determined creativity is perhaps the greatest legacy of the Harlem Renaissance.

Timeline of the Harlem Renaissance

1919 — Jessie Redmon Fauset becomes the literary editor of the *Crisis*

— Claude McKay's poem "If We Must Die" is published

1921 — *Shuffle Along* opens on Broadway

— Langston Hughes's poem "The Negro Speaks of Rivers" is published in the *Crisis*

1923 — The National Urban League starts publishing *Opportunity*

1924 — The Civic Club of New York dinner launches the New Negro Movement

1925 — *Survey Graphic*'s "Harlem: Mecca of the New Negro" issue is published

— *The New Negro* anthology is published

1926 — *Fire!!* publishes its first and only issue

1927 — Ethel Waters stars in *Africana* on Broadway

— Duke Ellington starts playing at the Cotton Club

1928 — Paul Robeson stars in *Show Boat* in London

— Bessie Smith stars in the short film *St. Louis Blues*

1932 — Augusta Savage opens the Savage Studio of Arts and Crafts in Harlem

1937 — Zora Neale Hurston's novel *Their Eyes Were Watching God* is published

Timeline of the World

1919 — Prohibition era begins

— The Harlem Hellfighters march on Fifth Avenue in New York

1921 — Dozens of African Americans are killed in the Tulsa Race Massacre; the Black community of Greenwood, Oklahoma, is destroyed

— Bessie Coleman becomes the first female African American pilot

1922 — The tomb of King Tut is discovered

1923 — The Charleston dance craze begins

1926 — *Winnie-the-Pooh* by A. A. Milne is published

1927 — *The Jazz Singer* opens in theaters. It's the first movie with sound and dialogue.

1928 — Mickey Mouse makes his first appearance in *Steamboat Willie*

1929 — The Great Depression begins

1932 — Amelia Earhart becomes the first woman to fly across the Atlantic Ocean

1933 — Prohibition ends

1936 — Jesse Owens wins four gold medals at the Berlin Olympics

Bibliography

*Books for young readers

Boyd, Valerie. *Wrapped in Rainbows: The Life of Zora Neale Hurston*. New York: Scribner, 2003.

Bracks, Lean'tin L., and Jessie Carney Smith, eds. *Black Women of the Harlem Renaissance Era*. Lanham: Rowman & Littlefield, 2014.

*Cline-Ransome, Lesa, and James E. Ransome. *Just a Lucky So and So: The Story of Louis Armstrong*. New York: Holiday House, 2016.

*Fradin, Dennis Brindell, and Judith Bloom Fradin. *Zora! The Life of Zora Neale Hurston*. New York: Clarion, 2019.

Hennessey, Thomas J. *From Jazz to Swing: African American Jazz Musicians and Their Music, 1890–1935*. Detroit: Wayne State University, 1994.

*Hill, Laban Carrick. *Harlem Stomp! A Cultural History of the Harlem Renaissance*. New York: Little, Brown, 2009.

Huggins, Nathan Irvin. *Harlem Renaissance*. Oxford: Oxford University Press, 2007.

Hughes, Langston. *The Big Sea: An Autobiography*. New York: Hill and Wang, 1993.

Hughes, Langston. *Poetry for Young People: Langston Hughes*. Edited by David Roessel and Arnold Rampersad. Illustrated by Benny Andrews. New York: Sterling, 2006.

Hutchinson, George. *The Harlem Renaissance in Black and White*. Cambridge: Belknap, 1995.

Lewis, David Levering. *When Harlem Was in Vogue*. New York: Oxford University Press, 1989.

Locke, Alain, ed. *The New Negro*. New York: Touchstone, 1997.

*Myers, Walter Dean, and Bill Miles. *The Harlem Hellfighters: When Pride Met Courage*. New York: HarperCollins, 2009.

*Powell, Patricia Hruby, and Christian Robinson. *Josephine: The Dazzling Life of Josephine Baker*. San Francisco: Chronicle Books, 2014.

*Rebel Girls. *Madam C. J. Walker Builds a Business*. San Francisco: Timbuktu Labs, 2019.

*Watson, Renee, and Christian Robinson. *Harlem's Little Blackbird: The Story of Florence Mills*. New York: Random House, 2012.

*Weatherford, Carole Boston, and R. Gregory Christie. *Sugar Hill: Harlem's Historic Neighborhood*. Park Ridge, IL: Albert Whitman, 2014.

Blues singer Bessie Smith

Sculptor Augusta Savage

Poet Langston Hughes

Performer Josephine Baker

Painter Aaron Douglas

Photographer James Van Der Zee

Meta Vaux Warrick Fuller's sculpture called *Emancipation*

Dancer Bill "Bojangles" Robinson

Author Zora Neale Hurston

Jazz musician Louis Armstrong (in the dark suit)

Pianist Duke Ellington

The famous Apollo Theater on 125th Street in Harlem

Members of the Harlem Hellfighters

Sheet music cover from Noble Sissle and Eubie Blake's *Shuffle Along*

The Cotton Club

Writer and political activist W.E.B. Du Bois
(standing, far right) at the *Crisis* headquarters

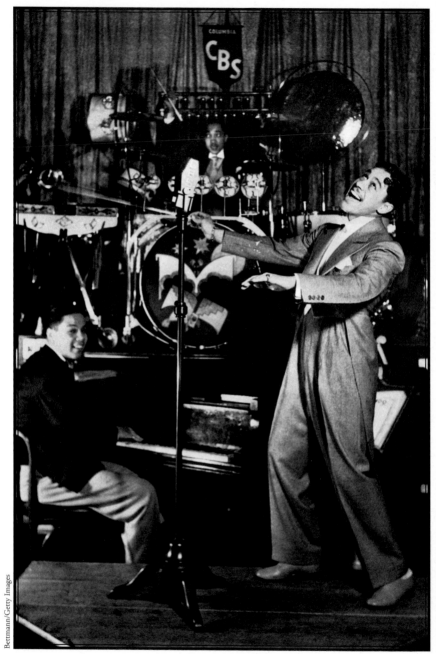

Musician Cab Calloway

Broadway actress Ethel Waters in the play *Cabin in the Sky*

Paul Robeson as Othello

Writer, editor, and critic Jessie Redmon Fauset